When Wounds Run Deep

Dr. Jeannine Mauwa

Copyright © 2023 by Dr. Jeannine Mauwa

All rights reserved.

No part of this book may be reproduced in any form or by any electronic or mechanical means, including information storage and retrieval systems, without written permission from the author, except for the use of brief quotations in a book review.

This nonfiction memoir is a personal account based on the author's experiences, perceptions, and recollections. While every effort has been made to ensure the accuracy and truthfulness of the events and conversations described in this book, some details may have been changed or omitted to protect the privacy of the individuals involved. Names, locations, and identifying characteristics of certain individuals may have been altered for the same reason.

The views, opinions, and perspectives expressed in this memoir are solely those of the author and the author does not claim to provide professional advice or endorse any particular course of action. Readers should consult with appropriate professionals or conduct their own research before making decisions based on the contents of this memoir.

This book is intended for informational and entertainment purposes only, and the author and publisher disclaim any liability, loss, or damages that may arise directly or indirectly from the use or application of the information contained herein.

To my children: My dear princes and princess, you are my greatest blessings and bring meaning to my life. You have stood by me during the difficult days, and for that, I am forever grateful. Thank you.

I love you. Always.

Contents

Foreword	vii
1. THREE CONTEMPORARIES AND A GIRL CHILD	1
2. THE SMOKE OF REJECTION	7
3. WHEN WOUNDS RUN DEEP	13
Separation Experience	21
Experience From Narcissist Relationship	32
4. THE PAIN OF EXCESS	38
Excess Trust	38
Excess Fear	39
Positive and Negative Power of our Tongue	41
5. SINGLE MOTHER	43
6. DO NOT TOUCH MY WOUNDS	47
Prevent From Recurrence	50
Persevere the Pain of Healing Process	51
Every Pain Is Temporary	54
7. TENDER CARE FOR THE BROKENHEARTED	57
Prayer Life Experience	57
A Friend Who Never Gave up on Me	62
8. LEARNED LESSONS AND ADVICE	65
Forgive Yourself and Others	65
Know and Understand the Time	69

Importance of Personal Meeting	70
There Is Always a Need for Planning	73
Focus	75
Do Not Give Up	77
Keep a Positive Attitude When Nobody Is Cheering	79
Place of Self-Care in Wildness	80
Kindness	81
Be Yourself	83
Confidence	85
9. MY WORD TO ALL THAT ARE HURTING	88
To Kids Who Are Hurting	89
To Abandoned Women	90
To Rejected Men	91
About the Author	93

Foreword

Sometimes, there are events we wish would never happen in our lives. Unfortunately, these occurrences often do not knock on our doors and ask for permission before entering. As a result, we find ourselves facing unfair situations. Accepting what is happening can be one challenge, while dealing with it positively is another. My experiences have taught me that darkness cannot withstand light. No matter how long it takes for the light to appear or where it finds you, it will emerge, and darkness will dissipate.

The objective of this book is not to accuse, expose, or vilify anyone, but to encourage and support someone who may be going through hard times and unfair situations. Darkness can befall anyone, regardless of age, race, ethnicity, location, or socioeconomic status. When we fail to understand or accept what is happening, the pain can devastate our hearts, emotions, and bodies.

I was born like any other child, hoping for the best before becoming engulfed in a whirlwind of darkness. For many years, I could not see ahead or feel the life around me. Whenever I stretched out my hand, I could feel a rough wall of darkness. Every day, I lacked hope for the next, but I kept going until the light appeared at the end of the tunnel. If I can be happy and enjoy my life today, I want to offer encouragement to those who are suffering. You will make it. You are not alone; I am here walking with you on your journey towards the light.

This book shares some life situations that I consider worth sharing, among many other sensitive stories. I am also sharing some lessons I've learned, which could inspire someone going through unfair situations. These lessons may not be perfect, but they worked for me. You can embrace some of them, dilute them, add an ingredient, or modify them to make them work for you.

Chapter 1

Three Contemporaries and a Girl Child

In the 1970s, three contemporaries resided in Belcon City, each working for different companies. Barbra, a young woman, lived and worked in the city, which was a four-hour drive from her home. As the third-born of nine siblings, she was a determined and hardworking individual, striving for a better future despite the challenges of living far from home without support. One of the young men, Joshua, also found employment in Belcon City after completing high school. Living a two-hour drive from his home, he too came from a large family. The other young man, Mathew, pursued a technical education after high school and obtained a certification. His skills made him competitive, securing an excellent job at a Belcon City company, which prompted him to relocate far from his hometown. Upon meeting Joshua and Barbra, Mathew proved to be a diligent and caring individual. Over time, he became attracted to Barbra, but when he learned of her relationship with Joshua, he respected their bond and remained a friend.

As Barbra and Joshua's relationship flourished, Joshua eventually proposed, and Barbra agreed to become his fiancée. She introduced him to her family, and around this time, Joshua was awarded a scholarship to continue his education abroad. It was bittersweet to see the two lovers part ways, hopeful that they would reunite in the future. Once Joshua left for university, they relied on letters for communication. In time, people began to wonder what had happened to him, as no one received his letters, even though he had sent them. Similarly, Joshua grew concerned, as he had not received any replies, despite Barbra having written to him. Unlike today, with the prevalence of phones and social media, communication was not as accessible back then. Eventually, Barbra felt left behind and soon discovered that she was pregnant.

This revelation was devastating to her, given the cultural stigma in her village surrounding out-of-wedlock pregnancies. At the time, such pregnancies were deemed intolerable and unacceptable. Barbra's grandmother, Lisa, had shared a story once about how unwed pregnant women would be cast away to a nearby island and left to perish. This frightened Barbra, who anxiously awaited contact from her fiancé. Distraught, Barbra wept day and night, fearing both for her unborn child and the societal consequences of her predicament. She began to suspect that Joshua had received her letter informing him of the pregnancy and had chosen to abandon her, explaining why she had not received any responses. As those around her noticed her distress, Mathew, a longtime friend who had harbored feelings for Barbra but respected her relationship with Joshua, approached her to learn what was troubling her. Barbra confided in Mathew, and they both feared the possibility of her being exiled to the island or subjected to unjust treatment. Barbra was already experiencing some rejection from society as they became aware of her illegitimate pregnancy. To protect her from further harm, Mathew proposed marriage to Barbra, who hesitated but eventually agreed due to their long-standing friendship. Mathew pledged to accept the child as his own, and Barbra, unwilling to consider other options such as abortion or suicide, chose instead to endanger her own life for the sake of her unborn child. She demonstrated remarkable strength, love, and humanity throughout her ordeal.

Shortly thereafter, a girl child was born and Joshua

returned unexpectedly. His arrival home was an emotional event, and he was shocked to learn what had transpired during his absence. Joshua sincerely apologized and expressed regret that none of his letters had reached Barbra, explaining that he had never received any correspondence from her either. After several discussions, they agreed to let the child stay with her mother for the time being. Joshua was expected to pay a price of apology and appreciation to Mathew, as per tradition, before he could claim the child. My grandmother later explained that in practice, a man had to pay a dowry to the bride's family in a traditional marriage ceremony.

Typically, the dowry would consist of one or more cows and additional gifts for the woman's family. If a man impregnated a woman, he was expected to marry her. If he didn't and the woman gave birth, he would need to pay a price to claim his child. This could be a cow or money to cleanse the shame he had brought upon the family and express gratitude for their patience and understanding, as not all families would tolerate an unmarried woman giving birth. As mentioned earlier, any "illegitimate child" carried the risk of the mother being exiled to the island. My grandmother explained that if the woman was married to another man who raised the child, the biological father would have to pay the price to him to claim the child. This was why Joshua had to pay the fee before claiming his daughter. After agreeing to do so, he returned to school.

In the following years, Barbra and Mathew welcomed a daughter of their own, Rose, along with two more children, Esther and Mark. Joshua, too, married another woman named Martha, and they had eight children together. As time passed, however, the situation became complicated. The initial plan for the baby girl to be reunited with her biological father failed due to mounting family tensions. Matters escalated to the point where the girl was forbidden from seeing or communicating with Joshua and his family altogether, as doing so would be considered a grave offense. For various reasons, the situation deteriorated further, and Joshua was unable to see his daughter until she began attending school.

Desperate to see his child, Joshua devised a plan to catch a glimpse of her. He would stand by the road she used to walk home from school and content himself with watching her pass by without speaking to or approaching her in order to maintain peace. But doing so proved deeply distressing for Joshua. One day, he changed his tactics and, as the girl passed by as usual, he called her over, quickly handed her a letter without much explanation to protect her from any potential trouble. The girl hesitated but accepted the envelope. Overwhelmed with emotion, Joshua hugged his baby girl and bade her farewell.

Tearfully, the girl returned home and read the letter:

> *Beloved daughter, I know you are going through a difficult time. Do not repay wrong with wrong, nor unkindness with unkindness. Act as if nothing is happening around you, allowing peace to prevail. Whenever I think about you, a force compels me to see you happy. I pray that one day we will be reunited. I love you and will love you forever.*

The revelation was a tremendous shock to the girl. Regrettably, she only saw her biological father Joshua briefly four times throughout her entire life. Even when Joshua passed away, the girl, now a grown woman, was unable to attend his funeral. May Joshua's soul rest in peace.

That girl child is me today.

May the soil be light on my dad's body.

Chapter 2

The Smoke of Rejection

It was difficult to accept that I was an illegitimate child. I fought against this reality and struggled to connect with both my nuclear and extended family. Doing so was difficult as I felt a force of rejection always pushing and repelling me away. Despite my best efforts – behaving well, being available, serving everyone, making sacrifices, and even foregoing some benefits to secure a sense of belonging – I still felt always undeserving. In the end, it took a great deal of time, energy, and pain for me to come to terms with my situation, and even then, I fought to keep my illegitimacy a secret.

As a young child, one needs the support and protection of a family to ward off various forms of abuse. This proved challenging for me, as I often felt the sting of rejection and resistance from those around me. I endured a great deal of hatred, betrayal, and exclusion, which proved to be traumatizing. Where there is smoke, there is fire, and I found myself surrounded by the smoke of rejection. I had little choice but to bear these burdens given the societal norms and traditions of the time.

In our culture, illegitimate children are often viewed as scandalous, subject to both passive and active aggression. Consequently, I grew up feeling devalued and constantly battled to conceal my illegitimacy. I faced numerous obstacles and was often taunted or insulted. I was called names, looked down upon, and traumatized. But whenever I felt overwhelmed, I would recall my father Joshua's letter and act as though nothing had happened, *in order to maintain peace*, just as he had advised. His letter became a soothing song for my heart.

I would reread the letter whenever I missed him, cherishing it even after all these years. I always tried to smile and appear happy, even when I was hurting inside. I did everything in my power to gain acceptance in society and within my community, but I consistently felt rejected. This became so commonplace that I would have been surprised had anyone actually accepted my efforts. It was difficult to find someone I could confide in about my struggles, as I had chosen not to divulge my tribulations in order to preserve whatever little peace I possessed. Society treated me unfairly in subtle ways; people mocked and whispered about me, and I couldn't express my pain because I felt so alone. I grew up with groups of young people who I could have been a part of, but I was deemed undeserving.

Frequently, I found myself at the center of local gossip. Determined to overcome this, I focused on excelling in school and maintaining exemplary discipline. My peers resented my academic success and often engaged in scandalous conversations about me. "She's illegitimate, after all." I struggled to find my place in society, and on several occasions, people bluntly told me to my face that I didn't belong. Everyone seemed to have something to say about me, which left me feeling deeply troubled and humiliated. I hadn't chosen to be born out of wedlock, and it was devastating to be called "a bastard" or any of the other insults people hurled at me. Even my own family members used my illegitimacy to bring me down and discredit me. I recall desperately seeking financial assistance for school fees from charitable organizations, unable to reveal my circumstances for fear of further jeopardizing my fragile sense of security. Yet, without this help, I risked having to abandon my education due to a lack of funds.

I couldn't live at home all the time, so I occasionally stayed with the same family members who didn't love me as I was an embarrassment to them. Despite this, I thought I could win their affection by working hard, but my efforts were in vain. I even went so far as to work as a house girl in an attempt to please them. As a growing girl, I needed more care and protection, but that was not the case. Moving between family members, seeking acceptance that never came, deeply hurt me. I needed attention as a young girl, especially when I began experiencing my menstrual cycles, but sadly, things didn't go well.

One scandal occurred when I was living with my cousin Elisabeth, her husband Eric, her friend Esther, and sister-in-law Linda. At 13, I was the youngest in the household. No one offered to buy me sanitary pads, so I resorted to using strips of cloth while my roommates all used pads. Everyone demanded an explanation when they discovered my washed and clean period rags hanging from the footboard.

I used to wash them and hang them to dry from my bed's footboard when no one was home and remove them before anyone returned. One day, I came home late after a group assignment held me back at school and found that my roommates had discovered my rags. Despite their cleanliness, it was considered a serious offense. In a house meeting, I was shamed and told to never do that again. I sought advice on how else I could dry them, only to be insulted further. The humiliation I experienced at that young age was beyond overwhelming. We had only one bathroom and no dryer, and I didn't have money for more cloth strips. What hurt me most was that no one cared to ask why I didn't have pads like the others. I didn't receive the same care and attention as my peers, and the situation felt deeply unjust. I remember crying almost to the point of collapse that night, and my tears continued for a week. When I recalled my father Joshua's letter, I decided to act as if nothing had happened. I wanted to die, but I consoled myself, believing that my troubles would end someday.

I endured a great deal at a young age, and looking back, it's a miracle that I am alive today. Yet despite the challenges, I continued to excel in school, hoping to graduate and reap the rewards of my hard work. I had high hopes for the future, particularly regarding marriage. I believed that through marriage, I would find the protection, value, happiness, consideration, and love that I lacked in my youth. I never stopped dreaming of a blissful marriage, which I considered my ultimate refuge from my troubles. In my mind, marriage was my only hope, so I worked diligently toward that goal.

I avoided any misconduct that might jeopardize a future marriage and focused on getting a good job after graduation to support my future husband and prevent financial strife that could lead to conflict. I did everything in my power to safeguard the future marriage I envisioned. Having witnessed my mother's struggles as a result of having an illegitimate child, I was careful not to involve myself with boys. I didn't want to inflict the pain I experienced on another person, especially my future children. The thought of history repeating itself, on top of my own childhood suffering, was unbearable.

Chapter 3

When Wounds Run Deep

I have walked in pain and been wounded during a good part of my life, feeling as if I were bleeding from within my heart. I have had to suffer in silence to protect others and everyone around me. Though innocent, I never chose how or when to come into this world. I went through unfair situations in silence, doing all I could possibly do for peace to reign. My heart regrets nothing I was supposed to do, which brings me peace of mind, a powerful weapon when facing hard conditions.

I was secretly miserable and felt sorry for myself. I decided to work very hard in class, setting a goal for myself to attain the highest educational qualification. I imagined this would be the only way for me to succeed in life, enabling me to qualify for a job and be successful. Though the external environment was not conducive to achieving my goal, I consistently got excellent grades in class. My focus was always on having a better future when I grew up and married.

Unfortunately, I jumped from the frying pan into the fire and my new experience as a wife was even more miserable than my childhood. I suffered beyond my worst fears and any scenario I could have imagined. My origin became a significant issue, and I learned that I learned that society did not wish well for me from week one.

If that wasn't enough, Nathalie, my sister-in-law, had volunteered to pay back any funds spent on me to send me back home to my parents. She even went so far as to suggest another woman to replace me. Being influential in the community, she caused many people to look down on me and fight for my removal. Leaving my marriage was the last thing I could think of, as I couldn't see myself ever returning to my parents' home.

I felt like that was the end of my life since I had always longed for a better life when I married. What hurt most was that the second rejection brought back painful memories and I found myself dealing with a double dose of denial. No one could possibly understand or support me, let alone stand with me. I didn't belong to any community, no matter how hard I worked to identify with one. It was beyond shocking as people I least expected made my life difficult due to their personal interests. It's not an overstatement to say that I almost committed suicide.

What kept me going was that I fought to protect my children so they would never experience what I went through in my childhood. I spent many years in that situation - too many - which was traumatizing beyond reason. I couldn't imagine breaking my marriage because I considered it my home and last destination. I didn't want to fail, neither hear nor accept the conditions at that time. Try as I might, I don't have enough words to express my sorrow.

After all I went through, marriage was to be my destination and refuge. I didn't want to fail in my next step in life. I did all that was in my power, knowledge, and capacity to eliminate obstacles that could cause issues in my marriage. Unfortunately, bad luck struck without warning, and things didn't work well. I suffered enormously in that marriage.

Despite my suffering, I decided to pay any cost to find a place in this marriage. I put in more effort to please everyone and tolerated things that ultimately caused my hopes to fail. I endured oppression, hoping to gain acceptance in this society. The new community's abuse grew worse, to the point of denying me the keys to my own house. I spent many cold nights outside.

One day we were left outside behind a locked house and kitchen. That day my children missed school and were deeply affected. We stayed outside without breakfast, lunch, or keys to the house. I asked my oldest son, who was five years old, to get into the kitchen through the window to get me something to cook for them. I dropped him inside through the tiny window after I removed the glass. Fortunately, he didn't hurt himself. Through the window, he was able to give me some potatoes and one small pot. The next challenge was getting him out. Since I couldn't easily reach his hand through the window, he stacked pots to reach the window. Thankfully, I managed to get him out safely. I cooked for them, and they stayed outside with me until nightfall. When the door was finally opened, they cried, and we were allowed into the living room, where we spent the night. All other rooms were locked. The resolution was for me to leave and never come back. It was a tough time for me. I remembered my dad's voice whispering to me again, "do as if nothing happened." I chose to stay patient, hoping for the best, while crying day and night.

I remember one day I couldn't access the main bedroom because the lock had been replaced. I never accessed my bedroom again. With a bleeding heart, I told myself, "You know you cannot see your marriage ending. You would rather have it sick but not dead." I then moved to the children's bedroom, hoping for better things to come one day. I stayed there for five years before leaving that house. What disheartened me was that despite my patience, I continued to face nightmares.

Another time, I returned home from work at around 6 pm and was unable to access our compound. The night before, I had been barred from entering the house until 1 am. I didn't want that to happen again, so I climbed a tree next to the wall fence to drop into the compound. When I got on top of the tree, I tried to step on a branch to reach the wall fence, but the branch broke, and I fell outside the wall fence. Seriously injured and with no one to take me to the hospital, I waited outside until very late in the night when they finally opened the gate.

I remember the day when I couldn't even access the children's bedroom and spent the night in the living room. In the morning, I didn't have clothes to wear to work, so I wore the same clothes again and bought underwear on my way to work.

My situation worsened when people from my childhood community got involved in my marriage problems. They were unhappy that I had married, and being the oppressors that they were, they would never stand by and see me successful in my marriage. Knowing what was happening, they realized I had no protection and joined forces with others to amplify my suffering. They would do things like call me, pretend to greet me, then use that evidence that we spoke to tell lies that I hate my in-laws. There was a time when they would come home and immediately leave whenever they saw me coming back. I wondered why they would do so, but I understood that oppressors never go on vacation.

One time, people from my childhood community borrowed money from my husband Gerard behind my back. Afterwards, I was shocked when my husband asked me to return the money they had supposedly given me as reimbursement. I told him I hadn't received any money, but he didn't believe me. He called our so-called "friends" to help us sort out the issue, but they had been corrupted by my childhood community and ruled against me. They claimed I had received the money and should pay it back. Despite swearing that I hadn't received any money, it was all in vain. I was insulted and called a liar and a thief. I realized that when my husband asked for the money back, they lied and said they had given it to me to cause me more trouble. They succeeded in doing so, and I went through a sorrowful situation. The next morning, I ended up calling the eldest member of the family, Brigitte, and explained the situation. I asked her to intervene in order for me not to lose my life over borrowed money. With the intervention of Brigitte, the family finally agreed to return the money. I was shocked beyond description.

All this happened in front of my children, causing them immense trauma and stress. I'll never forget the day I almost lost my child Emmanuel. I will never forget the day I almost lost my child, Emmanuel. I had only one assignment remaining: to fight for my kids in a highly toxic environment. I was in charge of everything. One time, my small, old car broke down, so I took it to the garage. I was unable to take my children to school. I pleaded with my friend Eric to drop them off in the morning and pick them up in the afternoon when school was over. I hoped my car would be ready the following day. Instead of dropping them off, however, he put them on a bus and didn't tell me. I would have looked for an alternative mode of transportation because they were still too young to ride the bus unaccompanied. On their way back from school, the bus dropped them off on the roadside opposite the house.

As they were trying to cross the street, my 5-year-old son was hit by a car, injuring his head. The impact dragged him to the end of the road, tearing the school bag he was carrying on his back. I couldn't believe it when I received the call to see my child in the emergency room. When I arrived there, I couldn't bear seeing him in such a horrible condition. He was bleeding profusely as medical doctors tended to his wounds. Overwhelmed by shock, I passed out. I couldn't understand how this could happen on the one day when I wasn't able to take my children to school. I realized how much they missed having protection. I felt guilty for not providing enough love and support for my babies. The blame weighed heavily on my heart and emotions.

My time in that marriage was full of sorrow, and despite all my patience, hope, and effort, I couldn't bear the idea of divorce. My health began to suffer due to my emotional state, and, when exhausted, I would buy a pill to help me fall asleep. I experienced irregular bleeding and trouble sleeping. I almost lost my uterus due to the extreme stress, and I bled for three years before and one year after losing my marriage.

The whole time I spent in that marriage was full of sorrows. Despite all the patience, hope, and effort I put in; I could not stand the idea of divorce.

I reached a level where I could not sleep at all. That is where my body suffered due to my feelings. When exhausted, I would buy a pill to help me fall asleep. I started bleeding outside of my regular period due to extreme stress. The time I would go without bleeding was brief. At times, I would experience my menstrual cycle as frequently as three times a month. I almost lost my uterus. I bled for three years before losing my marriage and one year after. I tried all the treatments but unfortunately, I could not get relief.

After five years in my children's room trying to save my marriage, things got worse. I had to leave for my life and my children's lives. Before I left, I requested a few more days to mourn the loss of my marriage. I spent 40 days fasting and mourning, but it was even harder because people around me were celebrating my sorrow and failure.

To everyone who contributed to the failure of my marriage, I forgive you. You were ushers to my destiny. To my lost marriage, I only say, "*a chaque jour suffit sa peine,*" (each day has its trouble).

Separation Experience

I would like to preface this topic with a disclaimer: my intention is not to encourage divorce. In fact, I personally detest the idea, having fought against my own divorce as much as I could. The purpose of writing about it is twofold: to empathize with people who have lost their marriages while pleading for sympathy when it comes to the treatment of divorcees. When I mention marriage here, I'm also including people who decided to live together and form a family, even if they have not had the chance to legalize it yet. For me, the fact that they promised love to each other and live together matters a lot, especially when they make the effort to raise the next generation together. These people are our sisters, mothers, aunties, brothers, fathers, neighbors, friends, as well as fellow human beings with feelings and emotions. All of them deserve our respect.

I strongly believe that when a man and woman decide to join in marriage, they should strive to form a happy family and keep it together. While there may be a small percentage of deviation, in general, most unions intend to live together in peace and joy. Agreeing to live together requires extreme courage to accept that the person you are going to live with is the best choice among your options in life. We all know that the decision to marry is not one to take lightly.

Marriage is a significant decision, as it involves the mobilization of a lot of resources to prepare a home for the new couple. It includes not only family members but also friends, colleagues, churches, government, and communities. Beyond personal satisfaction, when both the man and woman decide to live together, they feel the responsibility not to disappoint everyone involved.

They also often have expectations of growing together by having children, which creates a family.

Now imagine the circumstances that separate those two people and destroy all these relationships with themselves, their children, families, and communities. Their separation causes so much upheaval in their lives and those around them. Nobody would willingly deny themselves a good married life. When their relationship doesn't work, and they break down in tears, their hearts bleed at the prospect of divorce.

Although there are many reasons that can lead to this monster I refer to as divorce, nobody enters marriage intending to divorce. The way my society is built, it gives more credit to people in marriage regardless of how they are living together. Using my own example, I had some credibility in the community when I was still in the marriage compared to how I was demonized when I lost it, even though I was living in my children's bedroom and the marriage itself had ended a long time ago.

I know of many people who live in the same house pretending to be married but are really not together. They are in extreme pain and dream of a rescue plan, but they don't know where, when, or how it will come. I have known many people who lost their lives because they held onto dysfunctional and violent marriages due to fear of facing the stigma of divorce. The pain merely gets passed down to their children who are lost and suffering as orphans.

I have known men and women who have chronic diseases because of the disappointment and problems they are facing in their marriage. They too keep up the appearance that they are living together, but they are really not. Remember, these couples have extended families; their family trauma will affect their extended families too. Their performance at work will be impacted. When one partner harms the other, the country loses a person, the community deals with a crisis, and they end up with mentally ill children who experienced the trauma and drama at home. The performance of these children in school is affected, and teachers deal with their demoralization and disappointment. These children have other kids at school they call friends, and they affect each other when they share their stories.

First and foremost, I advocate for tolerance within families to create a nurturing environment that promotes mental and emotional health for all family members. In my view, the success of a community is built upon the success of the diverse families within it. From my observations, one of the factors leading to failed marriages is exposure to a dysfunctional family at some point in a person's life. This individual becomes "infected" with the "separation virus" and, without guidance or counseling, transfers this infection to their own family.

My goal is to encourage efforts to slow down and pray and eventually eradicate this separation virus, as its cost is immense. During the COVID-19 pandemic, I realized the power that resides within human beings.

Secondly, I urge people to be mindful of how they treat those who are divorced, single mothers, widowed, abandoned, and so on. Remember, these people both need and deserve compassion. These individuals would have preferred to maintain their relationships, but unfortunately, their relationships fell apart due to numerous disappointments, fears, anger, and wounds. They often leave their marriages and relationships internally bleeding, so to speak. Someone who has never experienced this might assume that the person did not do their best or is weak at heart. While I agree that weaknesses exist, one person's weakness may be another's strength. From my experience, most divorcees have done their best with what they had. Losing a marriage can cause immense pain and depression, which should not be used as a basis for insults.

Drawing from my personal experience, I strived for a successful marriage, working tirelessly to maintain it. I spent five years in my children's bedroom, begging for mercy, only to be pushed out and discarded along with my three children. Losing my marriage was devastating enough, but then people insulted me and kicked me when I was down. My pain became fodder for gossip all around, and people abandoned me, celebrating my misfortune as soon as my marriage became dysfunctional. I was labeled with shameful names and put through hell.

I want to take a moment to apologize to all divorcees, single parents, and widowed individuals out there for the difficulties they face. They are often called discrediting names, such as failures, useless, ignorant, incapable, unintelligent, powerless, and lost. I know this is not true, and hope you do as well.

We all face setbacks in life, and being in a marriage doesn't mean one has everything figured out. I wish we could all have it together, but the reality is that we often don't. Everyone is dealing with some form of struggle, be it illness, financial problems, family issues, difficult family members, or job difficulties. Despite these challenges, we are not useless to ourselves or each other. Every human being deserves happiness and success, and our goal should be to support one another in enjoying the time we have here.

I was once surprised to see my friend Ann excluding

separated individuals from attending her bridal shower, believing divorcees brought bad luck. I respected her perspective and decision, but it made me reflect on my own life. I realized that all the people who caused my marriage to fail were married, and I wondered about the forces at play. At that time, I was told I shouldn't attend a women's conference because I had nothing to offer, having failed to keep my marriage intact.

The reality of life for women who do not live with men has prompted me to include this section in my memoir. We have widows, single mothers, divorcees, and separated women, among others. I salute these women, as they endure significant rejection, hatred, insults, and injustice. I extend my apologies to them once again. It is disheartening how our communities treat them, facing rejection even when some are already dealing with depression from their loss. Please remember that they are not the only ones suffering; their children suffer alongside them. They shouldn't have to conform when their extended families label them with shameful names and refuse to associate with them. It takes considerable effort for these women to regain their footing and move on with their lives. Some may lose the courage to persevere. I recall that after losing my marriage, nobody wanted to talk to me anymore, as they didn't want to be associated with my failure and shame.

I felt utterly alone. They all left, calling me a failure, incompetent, and a source of shame. They insulted me behind my back, mocked me mercilessly, and expressed surprise if I managed to achieve anything in life.

I am pleading on behalf of divorcees, widows, and separated individuals who missed the opportunity to demonstrate that they also possess loving and caring hearts, desiring to keep their spouses in their lives as long as possible. These individuals are human beings, and many of them are parents. When you humiliate them, you hurt not just one person but also an entire community. Their children absorb all the pain you inflict upon their single parents. I call for assistance in developing strategies to mitigate the effects of this social virus in our midst. Please help me with ideas on how we can address these issues. Rejected parents lead to rejected, innocent children. These people are emotionally wounded and require care, treatment, and support.

When someone is dealing with an illness, they seek help from others. If they fail to receive assistance, they risk worsening their condition, potentially leading to death. However, when separated individuals cry out for help, why would anyone insult them? Sometimes, they are insulted even without asking for help, or simply for existing. We all know that marriage involves two people, and separation indicates failure on both sides. In most cases, the blame falls primarily on the woman, even though she may have wanted to preserve her marriage but couldn't because her spouse didn't, for his own reasons. The community demonizes the woman to a greater extent than the man, which significantly affects their children.

I worry about the kind of community we are creating for future generations if we fail to support those emotionally impacted by this virus. I want to emphasize that I am not advocating for divorce or separation. In my view, it is a virus that causes numerous problems in our community and requires a different approach. Based on my experiences, I consider divorce to be a cancer within society. I wish we could raise awareness of its damages and establish methods to care for those affected instead of insulting them. It is truly unfortunate that this happens to them and, especially, their children. If we treat people with kindness and empathy, we will foster a community of more mentally and emotionally healthy individuals.

People often mistakenly assume that when they insult a woman who has lost her marriage, she is the only one being punished for the unfair circumstances or injustices that led to the dissolution. However, these insults extend to the entire community. Just as an infection can harm the whole body even if it enters through a small area, the way we deal with or treat those affected will determine the overall health of our community.

In my opinion, the severity of the issue (in this case, divorce as a cancer) will determine the course of action and outcome. Proper or incorrect diagnoses also have a significant impact on the results. If the problem spreads to other parts of the community, specialized treatment is needed. While these individuals may be seen as blights on our community, the way we treat them will either worsen or improve our future, particularly as they are raising the next generation. The fact that they were unable to maintain their relationships does not make them failures. I know single women who have raised wonderfully successful children who have gone on to become doctors, lawyers, educators, and entrepreneurs.

The side effects of separation can be more devastating than the pain of separation itself. I dream of a world where divorce is seen as a cancer or virus that we need to address collectively. The world is still recovering from COVID-19, and defeating it required a high level of awareness, concerted efforts, and decision-making. It demanded teamwork, love, and care, along with the provision of resources such as medical equipment and infrastructure. At the same time, preparations were made in case another pandemic struck. Nations supported families that were affected. Can we offer similar support to those experiencing divorce? Separation from a person once thought to be a lifelong companion can be incredibly traumatic, and some individuals are left with severe depression.

Imagine the trauma a child experiences when witnessing one parent mistreat the other throughout their life or even witnessing the murder of a parent. This child is severely affected. Consider the feelings of a child who lacks necessities because one parent refuses to provide for them as a means to punish the other. These children, alongside their parents, become targets of scorn and lose self-love, esteem, and care. I do not judge whoever caused the relationship to fail, as the reason may stem from various unaddressed family issues.

If most divorcees suffer from depression, stress, or illnesses caused by substance abuse, there is a risk of high mortality rates and an increase in orphanages if nothing is done. Please remember that there are also those who suffer within their marriages. Our communities consist of parents and children, and the emotional and mental well-being of each member contributes to a peaceful and enjoyable world.

Experience From Narcissist Relationship

Rejection hurts. Everyone longs to feel loved, appreciated, and cared for. We all desire attention. I have realized that oppressed and rejected people often become desperate for relationships. In their desperation, they tend to welcome every relationship that comes their way, not realizing that not all relationships are healthy. Occasionally, we encounter "onion relationships," in which we shed tears every minute spent in such relationships. The longer we stay in them, the more hurt we experience. Just as peeling an onion makes our eyes water, these relationships are painful.

Excessive hunger for relationships opens wide the gates to our hearts, creating uncontrolled traffic to our emotions and feelings. This heavy traffic weakens our heart's ability to discern, and as a result, we may inadvertently welcome any type of relationship. By the time we realize that some people we opened our doors to did not deserve it, it's too late. They have already caused irreparable external and internal damage, exacerbating our vulnerability.

One of the worst relationships I have encountered involved dealing with a narcissist, who happened to be my friend Brittney. At first, Brittney seemed like a good friend. However, as time passed, I started noticing abnormalities in our relationship. I was always the one paying when we went out. We would agree on doing something, and she would not follow through, later claiming we never discussed it. She caused me to spend a lot of money on things she didn't want, without any apology. Everything revolved around her. She couldn't understand that my schedule could be busier than hers, especially when she needed something from me. She was manipulative and deceitful, creating stories to provoke reactions from me and then making it seem as though I was the one causing problems. Brittney was also a classic hypocrite; she lied for her own benefit and always insisted she was right. She toyed with my emotions to show me that I wasn't worthy of her companionship, belittled my character, and acted as though she knew everything. She made sarcastic, thoughtless, and meaningless comments to others in my presence. She always found a way to manipulate others to get what she wanted, even if it meant hurting those close to her, and did all of this without any remorse or regret.

It was difficult to deal with her extreme self-importance and self-involvement. Initially, I couldn't understand how someone could never be satisfied in life. I was constantly used to fulfill her excessive need for services, help, and support. It took some time, perhaps far too long, but eventually I began to notice that there was something profoundly wrong with her.

I was hurt by narcissists to the point that I started talking to myself. I almost went crazy, unable to comprehend what I was seeing and feeling. I have since realized that they are incredibly difficult to live with. Just as an onion shows no remorse when it causes us to shed tears, these individuals are mindless and unapologetic for all the chaos they create in our lives. I kept ignoring the first signs of confrontation, expecting things to get better. It was weak on my part to ignore the signals of dangerous relationships, until they began igniting fires around us. A narcissist can be a neighbor, a classmate, workmate, friend, mother, father, husband, wife, grandmother, grandfather, or aunt.

The damage is even greater when the narcissist is a relative. We tend to become aware of their emotional disorder only after calamities occur. Living with or being in a relationship with a narcissist is like dwelling in a mental war zone. You end up constantly exhausted, trying to anticipate the next psychological attack or manipulation tactic. I pray for those going through hard times to open their eyes and recognize the sources of their sorrow. I despised every experience I have ever had with narcissists. If you are mentally and emotionally fragile, a narcissist will destroy you. They are so slippery that it becomes difficult to pinpoint anything wrong with them. It's even worse when they are religious, as they use religious words to manipulate you further and cause you to make many mistakes. They are incredibly controlling, causing you to lose yourself. They want you to be who they think you should be.

If you have been hurt, please be vigilant. Flee from a narcissistic relationship, as it becomes toxic to the point where it can drive you mad or leave you mentally and emotionally unwell. One of the mistakes I made was trying to make them happy. You are responsible for nobody's happiness except your own. I went the extra mile to satisfy them, but they were never content, and it never resolved our issues. I apologized for everything and nothing, gave all that I could, and obeyed orders. Nothing worked in my favor. I wish I had known and escaped sooner. Based on the pain I experienced from narcissists, I have learned that I would rather be alone than be around them. When you don't compromise with them, they become worse and never change.

I tried several times to have healthy conversations, but in vain. They can maintain a normal conversation up to a point where they will suddenly switch when you least expect it. During that seemingly normal conversation, they unexpectedly lash out and twist everything you were discussing when you are unprepared due to the undeserved trust you gave them. Try to stay away as much as possible because they hurt you emotionally over and over again. Make no mistake, I have realized that they do it intentionally, fully aware of their actions. They are simply sadists, unwilling to acknowledge who they truly are.

When the solution involves distancing yourself from them, exercise caution as you begin to create distance. They will notice the loss of their power and start searching for another host to feed upon, demonizing you to everyone so that nobody will trust or approach you, preventing them from becoming aware of their behavior. Before you know it, you find yourself with numerous enemies, not even knowing when the enmity began. It is incredibly challenging to troubleshoot and neutralize their toxicity. They don't care about you as a human being; they care about what you can do for them. After causing chaos, they sit back, enjoy themselves, and watch the dysfunctional game they initiated. They can pretend to be hurting and in need of your help, only to laugh loudly at you when your back is turned. They are experts at being bullies and abusers, taking advantage of the trust they receive from us and ruining relationships. I had to let go of so many things to achieve peace, but it did not work. They dragged my name through the mud at every opportunity, speaking to anyone who would listen to them. I wish I had known about narcissists earlier, so I wouldn't have suffered so much. I pity those who have narcissistic family members, as I can only imagine that the situation becomes more complicated when it concerns a relative, especially a parent. I empathize with you because I know that you exist.

Chapter 4

The Pain of Excess

Excess Trust

I loved my cousin Rodrigo dearly and supported him in every way possible. I was there for him when he was sick, and I helped him financially with what little I had for his schooling. I even assisted him in his wedding, spending 24 hours on the road to attend and help with the celebration. I made him my confidant, only to discover later that he took advantage of my trust and used everything I told him against me. He knew my weaknesses and exploited them to create conflicts between me and various people in my life. I couldn't believe it.

There were many times in my life when I desperately needed help. It's not that I don't need help now—

we all need each other—but I was grieving from a loss and needed tremendous support. I thought I could trust anyone who offered assistance. The world is full of surprises, so don't wait to become a victim before exercising due diligence. I was hurt several times by the people I trusted the most, and I would react as if I were dreaming since I couldn't believe they could disappoint me.

One time, some so-called friends came to visit us. I left them in the living room while I went to use the restroom. When I returned, we continued talking as if nothing had happened. Unbeknownst to me, one of them had sneaked into the master bedroom and placed witchcraft herbs on the bed. My husband discovered them as soon as he entered the bedroom. That day, everything came crashing down, and I went through a living hell as I was accused of bringing the herbs into the house. It was beyond my understanding then and is beyond my understanding now.

Excess Fear

Human beings sometimes have a fear of facing various realities, such as falling ill, experiencing a bad breakup, losing clients, or having their business fail. Fear becomes worse when it affects someone who has experienced hard times in life. I've realized that excessive fear can cripple us, preventing us from working hard and moving on with our lives. When we hold onto fear, we become scared of everything. It's important to learn from the past and overcome our fears. Fortunately, most of the things we fear don't actually happen.

Recovering from abuse requires a significant amount of self-work. To do so, you need to think clearly, which can be difficult when consumed by fear. Fear often brings anxiety, which exacerbates our situation. I've learned that it's crucial to take time for ourselves and practice self-care. Sometimes we feel like we can't make it because we've tried and failed in the past. It's important to face our fears and overcome them. Yes, we may have failed previously, but we cannot be perfect. Embrace reality and live with it. Be honest with yourself about your feelings and don't deny that you are scared.

Envision yourself as a new person and cultivate positive thoughts that you will get there. Allowing excessive fear to take hold can lead to chronic diseases. Maintaining a peaceful heart is truly enjoyable. Let's rise above our challenges and strive for self-actualization or focus on a specific goal in life.

Positive and Negative Power of our Tongue

I couldn't close this chapter without sharing with you the power of our words. There were some sufferings I endured because of what people said about me. Some people abandoned me due to the rumors others spread. I recall one night I was forced to sleep outside in the cold during my marriage, all because of gossip. I can't recount all of the instances, but I did suffer because of some people's tongues. Sometimes, the person speaking about you doesn't even verify the facts first to determine if what they're saying is true or false. Even if it's true, spreading it could just be malicious gossip. I forgave them all because I was meant to experience the full extent of sorrow that was destined for me in my life.

I've observed various situations and continue to see how words and one's tongue can spark conflict among people. Gossip creates animosity and leads to rejection. I've also witnessed people experiencing injustice because of others' careless words. It's perplexing why someone would choose to be the source of another's suffering on this earth, where our time is short, through their words. Why would you make someone's journey more difficult?

I've learned that the tongue can be both helpful and

dangerous. I dislike speaking just for the sake of talking or discussing others without a valid reason. Some people even exaggerate when they gossip. While words can empower someone, gossip can cause their downfall. Refraining from speaking can sometimes save someone's life.

When I was mistreated due to gossip about me, I wondered why someone would volunteer to be a reporter of other people's lives. I couldn't understand why some people talked about others the way they did.

One significant lesson I've learned is that controlling one's words is vital. Sometimes it's better to remain silent. Even large machines in factories are shut down periodically for efficient use. This small part of our body, the mouth, should also be closed from time to time for the same reason.

Chapter 5

Single Mother

As a triple-wounded mother raising wounded, rejected children due to their association with my situation, I faced the most challenging task: dealing with my feelings and those of three other people. People around me exploited this situation to convince my children that I was the cause of their sorrow and that I had always been the one in the wrong. They used all my frustrations against me to separate my children from me, wanting me to be left alone to suffer even more. I always acted as if nothing was happening. I remember one time when those words troubled my children. I went on my knees before them, asked for forgiveness, and requested that they give me a chance to show them who I am on their own.

I could have argued, but I chose not to. I understood

the type of wind that was blowing. I wasn't supposed to engage in all the battles, knowing it wasn't the right time to prove my innocence. Although it was not easy on my heart, I acted against my feelings, realizing that humiliation for me was trivial compared to my children's wellbeing. When they grasped that, they agreed to start fresh and give me a chance to raise them, guide them, and be with them. I was overjoyed by their decision because I knew they were innocent and would understand better with time. Later, they witnessed many realities that helped them comprehend everything. I recall the day some family members gathered to officially announce that I should not consider myself part of them and that I didn't belong to their family. My children were present at the meeting. It was a terrible and unfair situation. The family members didn't care about my children's feelings and didn't spare them from the drama. I hadn't revealed to them that I was an illegitimate child since they were underage. They learned about it for the first time during that meeting. They cried profusely. To me, that was the final blow to my heart. I had grown accustomed to rejection, but I couldn't bear it happening in front of my little ones. That night, they asked me countless questions about their identity, which I couldn't answer. It was an immense burden to add to my entire life experience. Over time, they came to understand many things; we overcame the bad day together, became happy, and started discussing everything and making decisions together. They are now my best friends. I love you, my princes and princess.

Patience, sacrifice, love, and humility helped me raise my children peacefully despite the difficulties. There were moments when I had to seclude myself in a room and cry over my situation and circumstances. But once I had finished, I would gather the strength to rejoin my children and play with them. I cannot fully describe the pain I felt due to the consequences of my failed marriage. I went through rejection, trauma, and depression. I hated myself and lost hope. It was devastating to see the effects of my failed marriage on my children, especially after all the effort I had put into it.

My heart sank in the trauma. Until one day, I called a meeting with myself. I addressed myself by name and asked: "Are you done? Is there anything you can do to overcome your sorrows? Have you exhausted all possible solutions before deciding to throw in the towel? Do you know that you can live again if you take action?"

From there, I assigned myself the task of finding out what could bring me back to life, make sense of my existence, and light the way for my children toward a good and successful life. I wrote a new chapter in my story, set new goals, and worked diligently towards them. As a result, I am now a fulfilled woman living with purpose and my children who are enjoying educational, social, emotional, and financial stability.

Chapter 6

Do Not Touch My Wounds

I dedicated this chapter to sympathizing with people who have various types of wounds. Regardless of the stage of your wound, I empathize with whatever you have gone through that left its mark on your life. I would like to comfort you, whether your wound is still bleeding, covered, open, exposed, hidden, under treatment, or infected. Please take heart and know that healing is possible.

I went through challenging times in my life, receiving multiple wounds to the point where I couldn't tell which ones were bleeding and which ones were not. All I know is that a wound is incredibly painful, especially when it is exposed and open. Everyone can see it to the extent they're willing to. An exposed wound has a higher chance of infection than a covered one. All my wounds were exposed. People who had power over me kept touching them, inserting bacteria-laden objects, and even cutting to cause new wounds to emerge. I longed for treatment and dreamt of having my wounds at least covered, but unfortunately, they were only exposed more. From my childhood, I was hurt by the fact that I was a bastard child; I grew up in shame and rejection. I became an insult; I was told that I would not make it in life. I was not lucky enough to keep my marriage. I was called names due to betrayal, causing emotional torture. The people I least expected, especially family members, celebrated my sorrows. I was labeled a failure, abandoned, and humiliated beyond description. I couldn't hide my bleeding wounds. When you have an exposed, wet wound, you feel extreme pain. Whenever I tried to cover them, my own people would uncover them mercilessly and dramatize them without anesthesia.

I couldn't find help to heal my wounds. They became so painful that I couldn't allow anyone to touch them, nor could I touch them myself. I saw them becoming infected, and I started to see myself dying from them. I lost hope for tomorrow. One day, I decided to start dealing with them despite the pain. It was excruciating. Some were old and severely infected. It was not a pleasant experience, but I decided to confront them. Instead of hiding or denying them, I exposed them to get enough oxygen to boost their healing. It was not an easy process because it was the opposite of what had eased my pain before, but I realized that denying them wasn't preventing them from causing immense pain. The best preventive measure was exposing them. I decided to expose them to seek healing through pain, and today, I am healed.

To those who are wounded, I am saddened by your situation. I know what you are feeling. However, I have good news for you: if my wounds healed, you can be healed too.

We all get hurt as we go through life in different ways, by various realities and circumstances that leave us with different types of wounds, of different sizes and durations. Untreated wounds or improper care can cause serious infections, not only at the site of the wound but also spreading elsewhere. Even when we heal from wounds, we are left with scars that may also require further medical attention. A large scar shows how severe the wound was. I have learned that it is crucial to pay attention to our wounds and prioritize their healing before they become infected, spread, or become chronic, preventing us from functioning properly and stepping into our destiny. We are only passersby in this world; we will not live forever. The way we live matters greatly to our friends, neighbors, communities, and especially our generations.

Prevent From Recurrence

While on the healing process, I wanted to look back and identify the things that hurt me the most along with ways I learned to prevent them from reopening my wounds. It is easier to reopen a wound in a scar than it is in normal skin. I have come to understand that it is advisable to protect our scars as well. Please examine what is causing you the most pain and work on it. I came to realize that lacking something we desperately wanted in life does not change the fact that we are important human beings.

Likewise, having what others do not have does not make us more important than them. We are all important in life. We are here to help and support each other. If you were not given the assignment of raising children and never had any, you have other tasks to carry out on this earth. If you did not have the opportunity to find a spouse to take care of, there are other people and things you could care for. What we lack is not the only thing assigned to bring happiness to our lives. There is power in looking around and learning to enjoy what we have while finding joy in accepting what is missing. What we have is often much more than what we don't have. Please keep this in mind as we walk through the healing process.

Persevere the Pain of Healing Process

The healing does not come overnight. It is a process, sometimes long and painful. I have always told myself that if I endured the pain when I was getting wounded, how much more should I persevere through the pain of healing?

I persevered through the rejections I faced and kept pushing forward in life, even when it was so dark that it was difficult to notice even a small glimpse of light. My educational journey was challenging due to internal and external problems, but I endured the pain and kept seeking knowledge, eventually earning a Doctor of Philosophy degree without a scholarship. I endured the shame I experienced from rejection and the loss of my marriage. I endured the pain of raising children alone when children are meant to have both a mother and a father attending to their needs, helping them, showing them the way, educating them, and providing for them. Unfortunately, I raised them alone. I decided not to make it a war. I endured the pain, provided for them entirely on my own, and now they are happy, grown individuals.

Considering all the pain I went through, I resolved to endure the pain I experienced during the healing process. Do not give up. Keep going. Light will appear at the end of the tunnel. Pain during healing does not mean that you are getting worse; instead, it is a sign that you are moving in the right direction.

I imagined what happens to a patient with a very deep, neglected, long-kept wound when they visit a doctor. If the wound is bleeding, the doctor stops the bleeding. They cannot stop the bleeding without touching it. They clean it with different solutions to flush away any debris or bacteria. It is not a pleasant experience when they do this. If the wound is infected, they can apply antibiotics. Some wounds can cause previously dormant cancer cells to develop into tumors. Leaving our wounds untreated is dangerous.

In life, we can be hurt by the circumstances of our birth, the way we were raised, or the family we grew up in. We can also be wounded by the places we live or the difficulties and challenges we face. We can be hurt by failed marriages, or emotionally wounded by the fact that we cannot have children. Injustice, rejection, abandonment, or betrayal can cause us to suffer. If you are suffering, please take a step forward in dealing with your wounds; do not leave them untouched. Before, I thought leaving my wounds alone was a good way of dealing with my pain. Through experience, I discovered that I was wrong, and I had to touch them. Not only touch them, but sometimes I had to remove the scabs and apply medicine. Yes, it was incredibly painful, but I hoped for the healing that eventually came my way. I have seen people lose their limbs due to cancerous wounds. That is how we end up losing our identities, character, and even ourselves when we leave our emotional wounds untreated.

Be patient. Sometimes healing takes a long time, depending on how deep the wound was. It can require a lot of work. Healing improves the quality of life. Set new expectations as you go through the process so that you can see the small improvements and appreciate them. We experience resistance and setbacks as we move forward, but don't stop or revert to the initial stage—keep going. Practice self-compassion as an engine to push you towards healing. Take one day at a time, and you will get there. Accept your true self and imperfections, and establish your priorities and values. I know that going through this journey requires guidance, encouragement, and love. One of the purposes of this book is to tell you that I am here to encourage you.

Every Pain Is Temporary

I still remember the day my cousins called a meeting to inform me that I wasn't officially part of their nuclear family. Filled with anger and hatred, I was overwhelmed by suicidal thoughts. It was one of the last things I ever wanted to hear. I had worked hard to identify myself with that family, and it was difficult to accept the reality I faced. The rejection was intense; it felt as if flames were spewing from the mouths of people I had considered my close relatives. It shattered my spirit and my heart. The pain penetrated my heart and destroyed what was left of me. That night, I nearly had a heart attack after witnessing people I had loved and identified with for so long officially reject me.

It was not an easy moment to endure. I suffered from the pain, blaming myself and regretting ever being born. However, as I mentioned earlier, one should not give up on a bad day because as long as you are breathing, you can make it. I would have perished if I had kept all that negativity in my heart. Instead, I decided to shake off the dust and move on with life. I concluded that I needed to be alive to function, and I couldn't be active with a bleeding heart. So, I closed the door on everything that had happened, kept it closed, and started living.

I imagined an injured person who was bleeding; they needed immediate attention, or they would lose their life. That's why I made stopping the internal bleeding a priority. We often fail to recognize that when we are oppressed beyond description, our hearts begin to bleed. But since we don't see it with our eyes or in the mirror, we tend to let it bleed indefinitely. We don't give it any treatment or attention, expecting it to heal over time. Yes, it may heal, but at what cost? We end up developing severe conditions that lead to death. Protect your heart and take care of it. Everything happening in your life is temporary; even the pain will pass. I tried to focus more on other things and ignore the rejecting voices echoing in my ears. To stop hearing those voices, I decided to forgive them, even though no one asked for it. I wrote to them, "I HAVE FORGIVEN YOU. It was not you. You were merely agents to fulfill my destiny. I had to consume the full-sized cup of pain in my life. Have peace; I hold nothing against you all."

I felt more energized when I sent the message, and peace filled my heart. I learned to view the rejection I experienced in a different light. It was no longer just sorrow; I could feel a strong motivation and inspiration to live. From that time on, I resolved to comfort everyone going through unfair situations because I didn't want anyone to feel the pain that had once resided in my heart.

Chapter 7

Tender Care for the Brokenhearted

Prayer Life Experience

I was a small child when I started wondering about my future. I felt desperate in my situation. As time passed by, my future became an increasingly complicated equation. I could not see a way out. I sat down and thought about myself. I reminded myself that I did not exist by chance. I decided to call upon the Creator, who I believed had brought me into this world, to come to my rescue and solve my equation.

It had so many unknown variables that I could not imagine anyone else who could find a solution to it. I started fasting for three days when I was still a young girl, pleading with God for mercy and to show me the way forward without causing damage to my environment. I respected everyone's decision regarding my situation, whether they ignored its existence or overlooked it, sacrificing my feelings for their happiness, oppressing me for their appearance, or using my name in a negative way to gain credit, love, and more consideration. I understood that there is a God who surpasses all that was happening around me. I believed that He had a solution and would make a way where there was none. I saw His hand several times when I felt like everything was over for me. He always showed up with His hand raised towards me. The only way I could connect to Him was through prayer. I learned how to say all types of prayers. There was no prayer and supplication that I did not do. I especially loved attending prayer meetings when I got married and found myself engaged in another battle. It remained the only source of joy, happiness, balance, and comfort.

However, I started being prevented from accessing the house whenever I returned home from prayer meetings. Even if it was a short evening meeting after work, I would find myself locked out. It became complicated, and I began skipping some prayer meetings (although we only had a few) to prevent conflicts at home. I was a member of the prayer meeting at my church, "Overcomers Ministry." My leaders, Joah and Tirzah, called for a meeting to address my absences. I did not blame them for that because I belonged to that group and was supposed to obey all their regulations. The punishment was that I should not miss any other prayer meeting continuously for the next three months. That was not possible, given my situation at home. I had slept outside several times previously for attending prayer meetings. I did not want that to happen again. I sacrificed those prayer meetings, which were my only source of joy, to maintain peace at home. I wanted my children to live in a peaceful place. Unfortunately, that did not prevent my troubles from escalating.

From that time on, I learned how to pray alone. I needed God's intervention in my situation, which had worsened even compared to what I had experienced in my childhood. One of the things that surprised me was that the people I considered friends turned their backs on me and said that if I were a praying person, I would not have been going through the drama I was experiencing. They all abandoned me. Again, I understood them; I could not blame them because I, too, began doubting whether God was hearing my prayers. They insinuated that God was punishing me for my sins, which I considered to be genuine because, after all, I could not be perfect since I had read the scripture that told me that everyone has sinned against God and must continue crying for mercy.

There was a woman named Rebecca in my church who I saw as very prayerful. I thought she was more righteous. One time, when I felt extreme pain from my sorrows and rejection, I turned to God and prayed, "Lord, if my sins are too many to prevent You from saving me from all these troubles, can I at least look at Rebecca in my church? Will You save me for her righteousness?" She was not aware that I prayed like that. Still, nothing happened. I understood that everything has its own time. Time is important, and there is a time for everything. It was my time to cry and be left alone. Whenever I made phone calls to people, they would refuse to pick up, saying that I wanted to cry on them again. It was my time to lack, to live in hell on this earth. I stopped calling or talking to people for help, and I decided to fight in silence. I kept on praying no matter what I saw in my way. I had to seek God; He was my only refuge. I was alone, completely alone. I prayed when I could not hear His voice, without encouragement, and with no sign of anything improving in my life, but still, things continued to fall apart. Because of the darkness, I could not see any sign of help. I still kept praying. I love prayer moments. Prayer does not disappoint. Prayer works and is like a balm to our troubles. Now I enjoy praying alone, and I love it.

I would like to encourage those who are going

through hard times, praying and seeing no results. Just pray, keep on praying. Pray when you see your way, pray when you do not see it, pray during the night and during the day. Pray when you are alone, pray when it is not possible or convenient to pray. Pray when everyone says that you pray for nothing and when all conditions discourage you. Pray when you are awake and pray when you are asleep. Walk in prayer and sleep in prayer. I learned to exercise all types of prayer—solicitation, exhortation, and request—with nobody's encouragement. Do not give up. Something is happening when you do not see it. Keep watering with prayer for it to grow and grow healthily. Cover it with prayer, protect it with prayer. When my sorrow reached its climax, I could not see anyone around me. Some would be scared to greet me in order not to be associated with my problems. I only remained with God. God was the only one I talked to. Whenever I had questions, I asked Him. If I wanted to talk to someone and could not, I went to God and talked to Him about what I wanted to tell the person. I cried to Him. I talked to Him whenever I was hurting. I brought my disappointments to Him. I have seen that He listened to all my prayers.

There was a season during my battles when I became overwhelmed and could not find words to use in my prayers anymore. I would hide myself in a corner somewhere, bow to Him, and just cry or stay silent for the time I had assigned to pray, and then say "Amen." By the time I finished, I would feel a great sense of peace inside me. I have learned that we can find peace in the midst of a storm, that we can be comforted when nobody is available to do so, that we can walk when it is dark all around us and not break our legs, that we can have a destination in prayer in the middle of darkness, that we cannot be wet even though we are getting rained on, and that we can feel full when we are not eating. I was surprised to learn that God hears all types of prayers you present to Him. I do not have enough words to explain the power that is in prayer unless you experience it for yourself.

A Friend Who Never Gave up on Me

I have realized that friendship is a very rare commodity when going through a hard time. At the same time, it is encouraging to know you are not alone. Unfortunately, during my time in the wilderness, rejection and betrayal were my daily meals. I tried different ways to be loved, but I wasn't. I have come to understand that there is nothing you can do to buy love. The fact is that when it is dark in your life, it is dark. It is hard for someone to see you, and the few times that somebody might notice you, your picture will not look clear to people around you. I understood them, forgave them, and moved on. The more you fight for people to see you, the more ridiculous you become because looking at a figure in the darkness, you cannot tell whether the image is a person, an animal, an object, or a shadow. I understood people and refrained from blaming anyone and respected their positions. Buying love causes the wrong people to take advantage of your situation and misuse you while your heart has no extra space for any other abuse. You end up suffering more.

Some relationships are costly and poisonous, especially when it comes to buying them. It is better to miss them instead of experiencing them. Sometimes, when we get desperate for companions, we welcome different people. So, it is advisable to stay positive when things are falling apart. Desperation opens the door to anything; taking advantage of the status of your heart causes people who do not deserve you to enter your life and your heart and take advantage of you. Once you open that door, it becomes challenging to close it again.

I have known only one friend who stood with me no matter what happened. He stayed with me when everybody else abandoned me. He does not make a collective decision or seek advice from people to validate me. Instead, He comforted me through my journey. I am so glad that I encountered that special friend in my childhood. His friendship prevented me from taking my life throughout my darkness. He never gave up on me. He has endless love; He covered me throughout my entire life. He has to be a forever companion. If I didn't have him, I wouldn't be who I am today. He enlightened my ways when going through darkness. He held my hand when my footing became slippery. He hid me from the rain. He covered me when I went through life's storms. He healed me when I was heartbroken and gave me strength when weakened. He listened to my heart when I could not speak. He has always been a provider and protector. He gave me the strength to hold on during the bad days. His name is Jesus Christ. I can't prevent myself from thanking Him for all He has done in my life. Lord Jesus, I love You; thank You for never giving up on me and giving shape to this rejected figure.

Chapter 8

Learned Lessons and Advice

I have learned many lessons and will share some of them in this chapter that might help you. You may need to adapt them to suit your situation. Also, please feel free to share your experiences to provide solace to those who are suffering.

Forgive Yourself and Others

The only person you cannot get rid of is yourself. Being mindful of how you live and deal with your imperfections is essential. The way you treat yourself matters greatly. Pay attention to your thoughts and feelings about yourself. Treat yourself with care, as you are the priority in your life. Take time to learn, know, and understand who you are. I empathize with you because oppressed people tend to mistreat themselves.

What I experienced caused me to hate myself and I had suicidal thoughts several times. I didn't think I had any reason to live. I cried day and night. Being rejected for such a long time led me to deny myself. I had to reverse that mindset in order to start living. They called me a failure because I lost my marriage. The question was, did I lose it? If yes, did I succeed? If not, why hurt over that? It was difficult to accept, but it was the truth. I didn't want to acknowledge what was happening in my life. Denying it didn't mean it wasn't happening. Giving a fake smile was breaking my heart and I realized that living an artificial life hurt me the most. I didn't choose or enjoy what I went through, but it happened. I asked myself what was next and realized I needed a solution to improve my life.

Instead of fighting against all the challenges around me, I learned lessons from them to ensure I understood them better. I observed the puzzle game and learned from it. You need to understand the puzzle's overall picture before assembling all the pieces. My situation shattered my life into many complicated parts. It was even difficult to understand those pieces in isolation. So, I gave myself the crucial task of constructing the picture I needed to make with those pieces. I had to sit, learn, understand, and accept my self-image. While discovering myself, I realized that I was causing immense damage to myself by condemning myself for all the unfair situations in my life since my childhood.

One of the weapons oppressors use is to ensure victims feel guilty about every wrong around them. They will pressure you to the point where someone steps on your toes, and you end up apologizing instead. Despite all that, your feet can withstand the pressure, stay in shape, and remain useful. They always told me that I couldn't have experienced sorrow after sorrow if I had been good enough until I agreed with it. I was the cause of all my troubles. I have learned that self-condemnation ends up being heavier. One way I dealt with my situation was to accept myself and who I am. I realized that condemning myself was only tearing my heart apart. I resolved to forgive myself unconditionally. That was the first step I made toward healing. You cannot believe how much peace I felt since the day I called my name and told myself, "I forgive you." Regardless of society's incorrect labels, I gave myself new names.

Forgive yourself to the point where you maintain balance when things don't go your way. Understand and remember that in life, there is always a way out of all situations. If one thing doesn't work, learn and understand why. If it's because of your mistake, forgive yourself and try again in a different manner.

My key to such circumstances is to close the door on them, keep it closed, and move forward. Understand that failure, as well as success, are part of life. After all, you are a human being; we are all imperfect and can make mistakes. Forgive yourself and move on. The inability and failure to forgive yourself will hold your brighter future captive. Accept your humanity, forgive your mistakes, and move on with life. Forgive yourself, learn lessons from your past, place them over the pain, shame, and guilt, and then move on.

Self-forgiveness brings significant relief. It predisposes your heart to forgive others. Do not dwell on unfair things that come your way. Forget and talk to yourself about that. I used to speak to myself about what I went through, mention the name of the person who hurt me, and say, "I forgive you." Resolve in your mind not to repay wrong with wrong. Close the door behind it and keep it closed. The past helps us gain lessons and wisdom, not to be lifelong companions. Stay strong and plan to prevent what happened from repeating itself, learn from your mistakes, and move on. I resolved in my heart to forgive everyone who hurt me. I was carrying a heavy load by holding on to the people who had wronged me in my heart. From the moment I started the process of forgiving, my mind began to think properly instead of feeling sorry for myself, judging who hurt me, blaming, and regretting everything in my life. You are the only one in the best position to understand, accept, love, and have compassion for yourself. Forgive others for failing to do so.

Know and Understand the Time

In life, there is a time for everything. I observed the way we move by alternating legs. The left leg goes first, then the right for us to move. The same way legs rotate when we walk is the same way moments alternate in our lives. Happy moments alternate with problems, and vice versa. No matter how long the suffering lasts, it will eventually pass. Also, when you are happy, do not be distracted; save enough energy to make it easier when problems arise on your journey. That is why it is vital to understand your ripe time. It will help you know what to do, when, how to do it, and the possible expectations. For instance, if you are going through an unfair situation, you will be able to know when to talk, what to say, to whom, why, and when to be silent. Understanding the right time will minimize your battles and save energy to take you to the next day. You don't need to open any other door for a new struggle or fuel the existing battle.

I remember one time my battles escalated. This was when it was resolved in a meeting to prevent me from accessing the main bedroom in my marriage. That day, they changed the door lock on me. When I saw that I was almost exposed, I sipped a glass of water and kept water in my mouth for nearly 4 hours to remind me to stay quiet and not react. I did not see myself ready to be thrown out of the house with three babies. I had realized that the objective was to provoke me into a fight to give a good reason to throw me out of the house. Instead, I ran to the children's bedroom and kept quiet with the water in my mouth. I was able to stay five extra years in my children's bedroom. Neighbors who knew what happened to me said, "This woman who endures all this suffering must have no family to fall back on. If she did, she would have left a long time ago." After all that, I forgave them. I had to go through all that happened to me to produce the best juice of pain to feed my unseen person, to grow and fly to my next level.

Importance of Personal Meeting

In life, people meet for various reasons. They can gather to discuss problems and seek possible solutions or to celebrate their achievements. I had seen so many meetings about me when I was going through tough times. People met and decided for me. They imposed their resolutions and judgments upon me. Oppressors didn't consider me to be human enough to participate in their meetings. Several times, I was treated as an object. Whenever they did invite me, it was to ensure they humiliated me. I learned to remember which meetings to attend and whose voice to listen to in different circumstances. Abusers will try to silence your voice and dictate your actions until you lose sight of who you are. After long suffering, I felt I had no future. I couldn't even recognize that I had a reason to live. That's when I decided to sit down and call a meeting with myself.

 I reflected on my experiences, tried to understand my situation, and set objectives for where and who I wanted to be. At the time, I couldn't figure out how to reach those objectives because my path was dark, foggy, and windy, so I couldn't see or think clearly. Sorrow had paralyzed me. Personal meetings were crucial. From then on, I felt much peace and relief. I felt as if I could see better. Setting objectives gave me a reason to hold on and keep pushing for life. After that, I frequently met with myself to learn how to achieve those objectives. Personal meetings changed the way I thought about people and life. It became more about understanding myself than fighting to understand others and make them know me. I would figure out how to improve my situation instead of waiting for validation from others before taking action. The benefits we gain from knowing and understanding ourselves are priceless. Make time for yourself as often as possible because your resolutions override all other judgments spoken over you by other people. Remember, self-meetings will not prevent people from discussing your situation and reveling in your suffering. You will continue to hear their voices trying to bring you down. Do not worry about them, as you are a new person now with a destination. Follow your inner voice. Ignore their gossip and pursue your new dreams regardless of how dark your path may be.

Remember, enduring abuse is like being on a battlefield or in a war zone; many things happen. Protect your heart from failing as much as possible because it is your energy and power source. In a toxic environment, the risk of losing yourself is very high. Be mindful of that, take precautions, and guard your heart. Expecting others to empathize with you is difficult because they often won't. Most of the time, they will blame you for your problems. Do not waste your time fighting, denying, or explaining your situation. Doing so will only open more battles while you are already vulnerable. You will become exhausted from fighting too many wars.

Choose which battles to fight and focus on preventive and precautionary measures. Do not hurt yourself. Sing with me this song, "Nothing is permanent in this world. Your suffering will pass."

You will overcome it.

There Is Always a Need for Planning

I realized that we often fail to plan when going through hard times. Instead, we may convince ourselves that there is no reason for planning. This can be a mistake because resources to satisfy our unlimited wants are limited, even when we aren't experiencing hardship. I advised myself to have both short-term and long-term plans. It kept me busy working hard to try to attain my goals.

When hurting, we sometimes get discouraged and simply watch as time passes. I have realized that when times are unfavorable, it is an opportunity to gather all your hidden energy and capabilities to jump thousands of miles ahead. Make adequate plans and work towards them. We react differently to unfair situations. Some people forget themselves and don't care at all, while others try to show off, wanting to prove the opposite of what people perceive. They end up spending even the little they have on unnecessary things for their situation. It is crucial to have a budget when your days are dark. Do not spend for the sake of spending money. Remember, one of your objectives is to survive the rejection with little or no help. There is always an opportunity cost for every action we take. Be mindful of your spending. Plan for your finances, your sources of income, and your expenses. Financial imbalance will worsen your situation. That is why planning for every penny that comes your way is essential.

Also, plan for your time. On this planet, we were all given the same amount of time. The way you use your time is highly correlated to your success. Planning your time will save you energy. Remember, you have wasted time feeling sorry and mourning over your situation. It is okay, but that's enough. Now, stand up to redeem your time.

Watch your diet as you go through hard times. Have a good plan of what to eat and what to avoid. What we eat matters significantly for our health. Eating just to fill the stomach is not advisable, as you will become what you eat. Remember, you need to boost your energy if you are going through a difficult time. Plan ahead of time for what you need to eat, so you can get enough time to prepare it instead of just eating what is available, even when it is not right or affordable. It is better to spend according to your plan to help you spend less and save money.

Focus

I have come to understand that rejection impairs our vision. During my suffering, I could only see darkness everywhere around me. After setting my objectives, I started working on how to attain them. This required me to focus on seeing through the night to find directions. Due to many external and uncontrollable factors, it took me longer than usual to complete my education, even though I was bright in class. I remember the day I missed the last exam due to circumstances related to my problems, which forced me to repeat the entire school year and miss my graduation. I thought of going to the nearest forest and bringing an end to my life. I loved going to school and learning so much. Education was my hope to make it in life, with all other factors remaining constant. Due to various factors, I had put in too much effort and still could not graduate after a very long time spent in school. After the holidays, I decided to go back to school. It was never too late, and I managed to make it. It was not easy at all, especially since I was paying tuition all by myself. I had to hustle so much to stay focused and reach my goal. Today, I am a Ph.D. holder.

If I had lost focus back then, I would not be where I am now, having at least achieved my educational goal.

When things look down upon you, you need to look down back at them and take directions opposite to the ones they are offering. I realized that moving in the same direction as your problems is a big mistake. Life is about challenges; it requires enough energy to stay focused and never be driven away from our goals. Time changes; nothing is permanent, and you will be alright. Never harm yourself. The sun will end up shining in your life.

It is not easy to focus when we go through hard times, and it feels as if the winds are blowing our thoughts away. But no matter what comes your way, try to stay focused as much as possible. If you cannot walk, crawl towards your objectives. Don't lose heart even when your eyes cannot see; keep on moving. One of the biggest lessons is never to stop moving. Even if it means moving like a tortoise, move and keep going. I will cheer you up if you have nobody to cheer you up with love. So please keep moving towards your goals. You can make it. It is just a matter of time; you will get there.

Happiness and joy are possible with or without people who reject you. Do not die in the wilderness of this life. Stretch your eyes, look through the darkness surrounding you, and you will see the light at the end of the tunnel. I know it is not easy; sometimes, your eyes are tearful because of the wind and cold of nighttime. Focus. Keep on watching and looking. You will see the light.

Do Not Give Up

As you progress, give yourself ambitious and robust objectives. Remember, you are overcoming a significant obstacle of rejection; your internal, unseen muscles are getting stronger. Do not be discouraged by past failures. The past belongs to history, and you have not built your muscles in the past. Observe someone in a gym working on stretching and building their body. Forces emerge as the person pushes a little beyond their comfort. After some time, they transform into a different-looking individual. In the unseen world, you have been doing the same. It hurts as you work on overcoming rejection, abuse, and oppression. But remember, you are becoming a very different and strong person. Knowing that you are stronger today than yesterday should motivate you not to give up, even when your back is pressed hard against the wall.

I imagined somebody in a closed room at nighttime. Suddenly, the lights are turned off. This person's decision in this situation will impact their position, either positively or negatively. This person has options while in the darkness. They can choose to stand, sit, lay down, cry, call for help, or to move around using all other senses, trying to reach out to the socket to turn back on the light. They can try to get to a door to get out of that dark room. They can scream for help. I understood that whatever action they take will make the situation better or worse. I got inspired and decided to do something about what I was going through, even though I didn't have much. I decided to go back to school for a master's degree. I needed to be busy for a good cause instead of being busy thinking about my sorrow and, at the same time, sharpening my skills.

I had nobody to support me in any way. So, I took an extra job to pay for tuition. It was hard, but I kept pressing on and always told myself the light would show. I didn't give up. Before I knew it, I graduated. That achievement opened several doors to other different opportunities, including studying for a Ph.D.

Also, my Ph.D. opened other doors, and I am still alive. In my whole life, "never giving up" has been my motto. When your back hits the wall, please do not give up. There is still a way out. Do not give up, do not hurt yourself; be patient, as patience pays. As you continue moving, before you know it, your life will be restored, and your rejection will be history. When it comes to your life, it does not knock; it will not give you notice nor when it leaves.

Keep a Positive Attitude When Nobody Is Cheering

As mentioned, setting goals when we are still hurting is essential. Working towards your goals during dark moments requires significant effort. Despite numerous limitations, objectives are still achievable. They might take longer and demand more energy, but never give up. Several times, I found myself talking to myself, calling my name, and saying, "keep going, let's try it, we can make it, do not give up..." I would see myself through with immense satisfaction and joy. Do not judge your goal as too high to achieve or impossible before you try it. Try and keep on trying. There is power in attempting. This power is waiting to challenge people to push them to the end. We have hidden capacities that get released only when we put them to the test. Do not imitate other people's situations. Get inspired by what they have accomplished. But remember, you are unique and deserve peace of mind.

Develop a positive attitude, tell yourself you will make it, and work hard. Regret is one of the things I detest most. I fought vigorously to avoid regret in my life. Do whatever you have to do to evade regret. Regret is a potent ingredient for depression. Do not seek revenge because it will consume your heart forever. Instead, do things you can stand for and explain why you did them. This approach helped me stand firm with peace of mind and fostered a positive attitude in everything I do.

Place of Self-Care in Wildness

Taking care of yourself should be a priority for anyone in pain. I saw many positive results from doing so. It's okay to take some time off from everything. When you go through challenging situations, do yourself a favor and try to forget about your problems. Stop replaying unfair circumstances in your life. Listen to your voice saying, "I love you; you are not alone. You are a priority; think about yourself. What is your body asking you to do? What is your mind saying that if you do this, I will give you a break?" Is it taking a walk in the park, going swimming, attending church, getting some sleep, riding a bike, buying yourself an ice cream, or having some popcorn?

I have learned this, and it has worked in my life. When I felt overwhelmed, I would take a walk and feel better afterward. I would treat myself to a smoothie and feel refreshed. I would go to the park, watch nature, forget a few of my troubles, and become energized to face them again.

It's advisable to schedule time off for everything else except yourself. We get hurt and pushed by circumstances to overwork ourselves, which is another form of trauma for a hurting person. You end up being exhausted, less productive, and unable to enjoy your achievements. Allocate quality time for yourself while going through difficult times; it will ease your condition and help you achieve your objectives.

Due to an abundance of problems, I became addicted to working and forgot what was happening around me. I would get so stressed that problems and stress would make me sick. Several times, I went to the emergency room where they couldn't find anything wrong, even though I was seriously ill. Eventually, I decided to change how I lived and get some rest. From the moment I realized that I was the one who made my schedule and the only one who could adjust it, I became a new person. I learned that self-care is gold.

Kindness

When everything seemed hopeless, I often thought I wouldn't make it to the next day. When times are tough for us, they often reflect back on us too. Rejection can ignite anger within us, and our anger becomes a catalyst for hostility. When you experience this feeling, remember that it won't help you; instead, it will make things worse. Fight against that feeling and understand that it won't go away by itself if you don't resist it. Refrain from harming yourself, do yourself a favor, and be kind to yourself. Pay attention to what you eat, drink, and do, as well as where and when you do it. Location is significant; some places may intensify your negative feelings and encourage you to mistreat yourself. Being kind to myself greatly helped me as I went through challenging times.

It's difficult to be kind to others when we aren't kind to ourselves. What we feel inside often reflects on the outside, making it tough to control our emotions when we're hurting. Being a victim for a long time can lead us to generalize and seek retaliation against others. It's crucial to remember that not everyone hurts us; some people are innocent in our situation. Prevent yourself from seeking revenge on anyone, and strive to do good as much as you can. I understand that sometimes money is needed to show kindness to others. The secret I learned is that finances often don't cooperate with you while going through a difficult time. It might be challenging for you to be kind to others, but this lack of resources shouldn't prevent you from being kind. Do what doesn't require money. Use your talents, skills, and energy to serve others, and you'll be amazed by the results you'll get. Choose to be kind by all means.

I recall going through such a time, but I always tried to do something. For example, I would clean a neighbor's house for free. The neighbor's joy touched me and lightened my heart. I would feel different by the time I left that neighbor's house. My goal was to put a smile on someone's face even when mine lacked it. I had nothing material to give, so I gave what I had. Do what you enjoy, and volunteer whenever possible. Just don't stay idle—help.

Be Yourself

Oppressors weigh down our feelings to mold us into who they want us to be, to the point where we lose sight of our true selves. We should not constantly reflect on our lives and compare it to others and their circumstances. Rejection can make us feel worthless and insignificant. We may feel like we are living at the oppressor's mercy, devoid of identity or personality. Living with someone else inside you is one of the worst feelings I have experienced—long-term intimidation can cause victims to feel inferior to others. However, one day, I sat down and refused to be someone else. I took time to observe those who mistreated me and realized that some of them were more miserable in their own ways than I was. I discovered that they, too, had setbacks. Nobody is perfect, and nobody has everything together. I stopped comparing my life to anyone else's and moved on with mine. This mindset helped me run my own race and reject the burden of feeling like good things belong only to others. I began to tell myself that I, too, was deserving of peace, love, and a better life. I learned to live with my weaknesses and use my strengths, urging myself not to focus on my weaknesses since everyone has them, even our oppressors.

Take time to recognize and understand your strengths and use them. There is power in awareness. Sit down and assess all your strengths. Your heart will find relief the day you discover the hidden treasure within you. Utilize your strengths to their full capacity. Understand that rejection has the power to wipe out our potential. Be conscious of this, and be yourself. Do not get caught up or trapped in those lies. Listen to your heart and take action to improve your situation. Refrain from dwelling on complexities and learn to do something about the things you can't control. Don't underestimate any small action you take. Keep taking those small steps, and before you know it, your efforts will shine and light your way. Stay positive, be yourself, and do what you love. Take control of your life and allow your heart to guide you. Search your heart continually to better understand yourself. Be responsible for your actions and their motives, rather than blaming others. Your eyes may not see your full potential due to the darkness surrounding you, but that's okay. Focus on the small progress you see and embrace it.

Confidence

Human beings share common experiences, and believing that you are the only one feeling the way you do is a mistake. When things are not going right for you, comparing yourself to others and trying to match your life or problems with theirs is unhelpful. Instead, it weighs you down and creates low self-esteem. Remember that everyone faces challenges in life; what matters is how we respond or handle them. Rejection can damage self-esteem, but realizing that even the person oppressing you may have serious challenges can help prevent you from feeling inferior.

People around us may seem to have fewer issues because they choose to handle them with high expectations, which keeps their self-esteem higher. Adopting the same perspective can raise your self-esteem, helping you aim high even in difficult times. Remember, you are stronger than any situation you face, and nothing is permanent. It will pass, so take the proper position while you are still facing it.

No matter what you are going through, you can make it through. Whether it is an unhappy childhood, low performance in school or at work, or a dysfunctional marriage, keep your esteem high and maintain confidence. You are in charge of your life; take control of it. Be confident in your abilities and don't leave the wheel to someone else. Listen to that inner voice telling you that you are more powerful than you think, and allow your brain to release hidden energy and capacity into your body to drive you to success.

Be confident and trust yourself. Everyone makes mistakes, and nobody is perfect except the Almighty God. Learn from your mistakes and keep moving forward. When going through hard times, it is difficult to see even small positive achievements, but they are there. Appreciate every positive step you make and celebrate the little good things in your life. Believe in those small steps and keep going. Be confident that you can accomplish even greater things. Once you boost your self-esteem, you will improve your relationship with yourself and feel healthier, opening greater doors to success.

Instead of focusing solely on your suffering, problems, and rejection, look around you in two different ways. First, recognize the positive aspects of your life, no matter how small, and appreciate them. The more you look for positive things in your life, the more significant and prominent they will become. This renewed energy will help you overcome depression, anger, sorrow, and disappointment. Second, observe the people around you who may be suffering more than you. As you focus on others and open your mind, you will see the capacity within you to help them.

Serve and help others without expecting anything in return. This can bring you much joy and contribute to your healing. Understand that self-appreciation plays a huge role in opening new paths to success. Appreciating your efforts can help guard your heart against further disappointment.

Stay positive and work hard. One mistake many people make is abandoning themselves during times of rejection. Take time for self-care and regain confidence in yourself. If you need to visit the past, focus on good memories. They are there, and they serve as significant resources for today and tomorrow's success.

Chapter 9

My Word to All That Are Hurting

Dear friends and readers, we are all on this earth for a limited time; we are merely passing through. What matters is not how we arrive or depart, but whether we have truly lived. Helping someone in need is invaluable, and making peace is a priceless act. I've included this chapter to challenge everyone to bring smiles to the faces of those in pain, as often as possible. Each action we take has an opportunity cost, so let us choose to live in unity and love. Let's stand together against anything that divides us. When we live in harmony, we succeed and celebrate together. I fervently pray for love among us. Forgive those who hurt you, assist those in need, and celebrate one another. Everyone on this planet has value, a purpose, an identity, a destiny, and a right to life. After all, no one can take another's success, blessings, destiny, or life.

I implore you to show special love and attention to abandoned children who are suffering and lost. Let's hold their hands and guide them safely to their destiny. Help them see that life is possible even when they are surrounded by darkness. Let us be beacons of light, illuminating their paths with our love, because even if we don't, light will still find a way to shine on their journey.

To Kids Who Are Hurting

I am here to console you. Please stop crying. Yes, things are tough, I know; but do me a favor and stop crying for a moment. I have some words for you: You are mighty; you can do anything you decide to do and become someone if you want to. If you still have a blank page on which to write a new story, do not give up. What happened is now history; do not dwell on it. Do not blame yourself or anybody for your suffering. It's okay. They did it, but they did not take your destiny. Now is not the time for blame. It is time to stand up, compose your new story. Take a pen, write it, and actualize it. As long as you are still alive, you have all the potential to create a new you. Please set a new goal; let me hold your hand, and together we can make it. Look at your potential. Release that and allow it to work for you. I know it is hard, but you will make it. If I made it, you can make it too. You are unique; you are not like others, and you are not someone else; you are you. Please take the first step and the rest will follow. Keep going. Keep crawling if you cannot walk. I see you walking; I see you running. I see you touching your destiny. I see you holding your success. Do not release it. Hold on tight.

To Abandoned Women

Where are you? Please listen to this little voice whispering in your ears, saying, "You are so special; do not give up. You have made it this far; you are heroes, you are beautiful, and you are strong." You have not allowed yourself to be defeated by all that you are going through. You are heroes because you still fight for yourself and your beloved children. Your special love, care, and sacrifice for others are your strength. I want to thank you from the bottom of my heart. You are not alone. I know what you are feeling. Guess what? You will make it. Please search within yourself; you will find incredible energy hidden inside you. Release it from your heart to help you leap over this dark valley. Try! You have it. You can make it. Let us go, let us move on, let us keep our spirits burning, whatever happened or is still happening. There is light at the end of the tunnel. Darkness never withstands light. Look up; your success is calling you. Let us walk towards it. Let's work for it.

To Rejected Men

You are a strong creature facing the reality of life. Sometimes, things don't go the way we want them to. Unfair situations, setbacks, and bad breaks happen. At times, we hide our emotions, and it remains unknown that we are suffering. We should not allow our sons, brothers, uncles, husbands, friends, or colleagues to suffer from heartache due to accumulated pain. We, your brothers, friends, colleagues, sisters, and mothers, are here to stand with you and support you. Do not suffer in silence alone and do not be ashamed. You will overcome it. It is part of life. I advise you to close the door on all the situations troubling you and keep them closed forever. Instead, raise your head and see a leader there, that little light showing your way. It just needs your eye contact to come your way. When you are not allowed to stand up, it is just a matter of life. Time will come when you will look back and miss all that is chasing you. Nothing is permanent under the sun; another time is on its way and ready to embrace the light it carries. If you stay in that bondage, it will bypass you because you will not have developed those characteristics that attract life.

To everyone else going through unfair situations, I wish you peace and love.

About the Author

Dr. Jeannine Mauwa is a distinguished professor of Economics, accomplished researcher, data analyst, and consultant specializing in corporate finance. With an extensive background in corporate financing and reporting, taxation, proposal and procedure manual writing, and business planning, she has developed expertise in Medical and Dental Billing, Asset Management, Strategic Management, Budgeting, and Management Information Systems.

Dr. Mauwa earned her Ph.D. in Business Administration-Finance, an MBA in Banking and Finance, and a bachelor's degree in Economics. She possesses a CPA I certification and has completed training in tax preparation, IFRS (International Financial Reporting Standards), Management Control Techniques, Auditing and Control Techniques, and IT Business Organization and Control.

In addition to her impressive academic credentials, Dr. Mauwa is well-versed in various professional software applications, including QuickBooks, Sage, Expert, Cash, Avionte, Prism HR-payroll, SPSS, Medoffice, Dentoffice, Canvas, Peoplesoft, Moodle, and OBS (Open Broadcaster Software). With her vast knowledge and experience, Dr. Mauwa's memoir promises to offer valuable insights into the world of economics and finance.

Made in the USA
Columbia, SC
01 April 2024